This Book Belongs To:

Let's Learn the Letter A!

Step 1: Trace the Big A and Little a

A A A A A A

a a a a a a a

Step 2: Try Writing It on Your Own!

– – – – – – – – –

– – – – – – – – –

Step 3: Find the A's! Circle them:

A B a C D A E a F G A H a I J

Fun Fact from Snookie:

A is for Apple, Ant, and Alligator!

Let's Learn the Letter B!

<u>Step 1:</u> Trace the Big B and Little b

B B B B B B

b b b b b b b

<u>Step 2:</u> Try Writing It on Your Own!

- - - - - - -

- - - - - - -

<u>Step 3:</u> Find the B's! Circle them:

X b V Z g R s B F Y N q b U B E B z B x b G B

<u>Fun Fact from Otto:</u>

<u>B</u> is for Ball, Bee & Blue!

Let's Learn the Letter C!

Step 1: Trace the Big C and Little c

C C C C C C

c c c c c c c

Step 2: Try Writing It on Your Own!

— — — — — — — —

— — — — — — — —

Step 3: Find the C's! Circle them:

y d C H u V t c j C I I C J j c g C m s W C i c

Fun Fact from Otto:

<u>C</u> is for Cat, Car & Cake!

Let's Learn the Letter D!

Step 1: Trace the Big D and Little d

D D D D D D

d d d d d d

Step 2: Try Writing It on Your Own!

- - - - - - - -

- - - - - - - -

Step 3: Find the D's! Circle them:

R d p X J M D M z F u Q q z D S B D F O V

Fun Fact from Snookie:

D is for Dog, Drum & Duck!

Let's Learn the Letter E!

Step 1: Trace the Big E and Little e

E E E E E E

e e e e e e e

Step 2: Try Writing It on Your Own!

_ _ _ _ _ _ _ _

_ _ _ _ _ _ _ _

Step 3: Find the E's! Circle them:

D m e x E B Z l e E X E q F x i O S e K E X W

Fun Fact from Otto:

E is for Elephant, Egg & Eagle!

Let's Learn the Letter F!

Step 1: Trace the Big F and Little f

F F F F F F

f f f f f f f

Step 2: Try Writing It on Your Own!

— — — — — — — —

— — — — — — — —

Step 3: Find the F's! Circle them:

a F s d F e f e F V t f F C B g f L U J h J f u F

Fun Fact from Snookie:

F is for Fish, Frog & Feather!

Let's Learn the Letter G!

Step 1: Trace the Big G and Little g

G G G G G G

g g g g g g g

Step 2: Try Writing It on Your Own!

— — — — — — — —

— — — — — — — —

Step 3: Find the G's! Circle them:

G e G O I G g q R T g I R G R N v G g B d x P

Fun Fact from Otto:

<u>G</u> is for Goat, Green & Guitar!

Let's Learn the Letter H!

Step 1: Trace the Big H and Little h

H H H H H H

h h h h h h h

Step 2: Try Writing It on Your Own!

- - - - - - - - -

- - - - - - - - -

Step 3: Find the H's! Circle them:

b f Q h g y E t s r E E H Y h H o h X H e O j

Fun Fact from Otto:

<u>H</u> is for Horse, Hat & House!

Let's Learn the Letter I!

Step 1: Trace the Big I and Little i

I I I I I I

i i i i i i i i

Step 2: Try Writing It on Your Own!

- - - - - - - -

- - - - - - - -

Step 3: Find the I's! Circle them:

v r Z i y a m I i b J t T I y L i H I u r i y F I

Fun Fact from Otto:

I is for Igloo, Ink & Ice cream!

Let's Learn the Letter J!

Step 1: Trace the Big J and Little j

J J J J J J

j j j j j j j

Step 2: Try Writing It on Your Own!

- - - - - - - -

- - - - - - - -

Step 3: Find the J's! Circle them:

N Z j I J A j B m z M D J x E Y B j J O D K r

Fun Fact from Snookie:

J is for Jumper, Jelly & Jam!

Let's Learn the Letter K!

Step 1: Trace the Big K and Little k

K K K K K K

k k k k k k k

Step 2: Try Writing It on Your Own!

— — — — — — — —

— — — — — — — —

Step 3: Find the K's! Circle them:

K e R k o H K k E K E v k z c Y P g i V F Y K v R

Fun Fact from Otto:

K is for Kangaroo, Kite & Koala!

Let's Learn the Letter L!

Step 1: Trace the Big L and Little l

L L L L L L

l l l l l l l l

Step 2: Try Writing It on Your Own!

— — — — — — — —

— — — — — — — —

Step 3: Find the L's! Circle them:

D a L e g V l x L H l e r j w a l Q S L c l T L P

Fun Fact from Otto:

L is for Lion, Ladder & Lollipop!

Let's Learn the Letter M!

Step 1: Trace the Big M and Little m

M M M M M M

m m m m m m

Step 2: Try Writing It on Your Own!

- - - - - - - -

- - - - - - - -

Step 3: Find the M's! Circle them:

N M Q j m N m o E X M F r W C m N K T M Z

Fun Fact from Snookie:

M is for Monkey, Moon & Mouse!

Let's Learn the Letter N!

Step 1: Trace the Big N and Little n

N N N N N N

n n n n n n

Step 2: Try Writing It on Your Own!

- - - - - - - -

- - - - - - - -

Step 3: Find the N's! Circle them:

N G x d c N i e n e n E t V V b N k n I M N T

Fun Fact from Otto:

N is for Nose, Nest & Net!

Let's Learn the Letter O!

Step 1: Trace the Big O and Little o

O O O O O O

o o o o o o o

Step 2: Try Writing It on Your Own!

- - - - - - - -

- - - - - - - -

Step 3: Find the O's! Circle them:

Y a o O g o z j U O Q G n p o U r P O c k o M

Fun Fact from Otto:

O is for Octopus, Owl, Orange & Otto!

Let's Learn the Letter P!

Step 1: Trace the Big P and Little p

P P P P P P

p p p p p p p

Step 2: Try Writing It on Your Own!

- - - - - - -

- - - - - - -

Step 3: Find the P's! Circle them:

E I P U x P z l K p B b g p p f A x P Z P e r p k

Fun Fact from Snookie:

P is for Pink, Pencil & Penguin!

Let's Learn the Letter Q!

Step 1: Trace the Big Q and Little q

Q Q Q Q Q Q

q q q q q q q

Step 2: Try Writing It on Your Own!

‐ ‐ ‐ ‐ ‐ ‐ ‐ ‐ ‐

‐ ‐ ‐ ‐ ‐ ‐ ‐ ‐ ‐

Step 3: Find the Q's! Circle them:

Q x q E Y q E A G R C Q Z i k M g X Q q d Q

Fun Fact from Otto:

Q is for Queen, Quilt & Quack Quack!

Let's Learn the Letter R!

Step 1: Trace the Big R and Little r

R R R R R R

r r r r r r r

Step 2: Try Writing It on Your Own!

– – – – – – – –

– – – – – – – –

Step 3: Find the R's! Circle them:

R y Q k O T R j r K c F R r D R L J g N r Z K p

Fun Fact from Snookie:

R is for Rabbit, Red & Rainbow!

Let's Learn the Letter S!

Step 1: Trace the Big S and Little s

S S S S S

s s s s s s s

Step 2: Try Writing It on Your Own!

— — — — — — — — —

— — — — — — — — —

Step 3: Find the S's! Circle them:

T p N X S n u c s b Q k s t N m X S l G Y C S

Fun Fact from Otto:

S is for Snail, Sun Snake & Snookie !

Let's Learn the Letter T!

Step 1: Trace the Big T and Little t

T T T T T T

t t t t t t t

Step 2: Try Writing It on Your Own!

- - - - - - - -

- - - - - - - -

Step 3: Find the T's! Circle them:

v t M e T x w W t r T T H t p T m z R j n I E

Fun Fact from Otto:

T is for Tiger, Train & Tree!

Let's Learn the Letter U!

Step 1: Trace the Big U and Little u

U U U U U U

u u u u u u

Step 2: Try Writing It on Your Own!

--- --- --- --- --- --- --- ---

--- --- --- --- --- --- --- ---

Step 3: Find the U's! Circle them:

A U c D C j j U u g m p P U I z l U R u k p u q

Fun Fact from Otto:

U is for Umbrella, Unicorn & Uniform!

Let's Learn the Letter V!

Step 1: Trace the Big V and Little v

V V V V V V

v v v v v v v

Step 2: Try Writing It on Your Own!

— — — — — — — —

— — — — — — — —

Step 3: Find the V's! Circle them:

c B J h v V H v V g R V q Q x V p V W T w

Fun Fact from Snookie:

V is for Violin, Volcano & Van!

Let's Learn the Letter W!

Step 1: Trace the Big W and Little w

W W W W W W

w w w w w w w

Step 2: Try Writing It on Your Own!

— — — — — — — —

— — — — — — — —

Step 3: Find the W's! Circle them:

Z w R r b x W g v W x W w l P X D w F O u

Fun Fact from Snookie:

W is for Whale, Wolf & Watermelon!

Let's Learn the Letter X!

<u>Step 1</u>: Trace the Big X and Little x

X X X X X X

x x x x x x x

<u>Step 2</u>: Try Writing It on Your Own!

- - - - - - - - -

- - - - - - - - -

<u>Step 3</u>: Find the X's! Circle them:

O k x W e P U X R X h y x e X R s x O A X g

<u>Fun Fact from Otto</u>:

<u>X</u> is for X-ray & Xylophone!

Let's Learn the Letter Y!

Step 1: Trace the Big Y and Little y

Y Y Y Y Y Y

Y Y Y Y Y Y Y

Step 2: Try Writing It on Your Own!

— — — — — — — —

— — — — — — — —

Step 3: Find the Y's! Circle them:

y C H x y Z c Y m H e y x Y W Z g Y m K J y e

Fun Fact from Snookie:

Y is for Yellow, Yummy & Yo-yo!

Let's Learn the Letter Z!

Step 1: Trace the Big Z and Little z

Z Z Z Z Z Z

Z Z Z Z Z Z Z

Step 2: Try Writing It on Your Own!

‒ ‒ ‒ ‒ ‒ ‒ ‒ ‒ ‒

‒ ‒ ‒ ‒ ‒ ‒ ‒ ‒ ‒

Step 3: Find the Z's! Circle them:

h z p K x Z l o Z X Z n x n D z Q H F K z Z m

Fun Fact from Snookie:

Z is for Zebra, Zipper & Zoo!

You have finished.

Well done.

Snookie's notes and pictures

Otto's notes and pictures